Donated to

SAINT PAUL PUBLIC LIBRARY

Monica Ochtrup

WHAT I CANNOT SAY/I WILL SAY

WHAT I CANNOT SAY/
I WILL SAY

Monica Ochtrup

with graphics by
Elizabeth Erickson

Minnesota Voices Project #22

New Rivers Press 1984

copyright © 1984 by Monica Ochtrup and Elizabeth Erickson
Library of Congress Catalog Card Number: 84-061825
ISBN 0-89823-059-4
All rights reserved
Book Design: Daren Sinsheimer and C. W. Truesdale
Typesetting: Peregrine Cold Type
Author photo by Bob Ochtrup
Cover photo: Steve Niedorf

Some of the poems in *What I Cannot Say/I Will Say* first appeared in the following publications: *Lake Street Review, Selby-Lake Bus* (anthology), *WARM Journal, Great River Review, Studio One, Sing Heavenly Muse!*, and *A Change In Weather*. Our thanks to the editors of these publications for permission to reprint here. The author also wishes to thank Deborah Keenan for her invaluable assistance in editing this book. The cover and inside art work by Elizabeth Erickson is from her series of paintings, *Temples to the Ebb and Flow*.

What I Cannot Say/I Will Say has been published with the aid of grants from the Jerome Foundation, the Dayton Hudson Foundation (with funds provided by B. Dalton, Bookseller), the First Bank System Foundation, the United Arts Fund (with funds provided in part by the McKnight Foundation), and the Metropolitan Regional Arts Council (with funds appropriated by the Minnesota State Legislature).

New Rivers Press books are distributed by:

Small Press Distribution, Inc.   Bookslinger
1784 Shattuck Ave.   213 East 4th St.
Berkeley, CA 94709   St. Paul, MN 55101

What I Cannot Say/I Will Say has been manufactured in the United States of America for New Rivers Press, Inc. (C. W. Truesdale, editor/publisher), 1602 Selby Ave., St. Paul, MN 55104 in a first edition of 1000 copies.

For my grandma, Anna

With grateful acknowledgment

To Elizabeth, Joyce, and Delor
Without whom I might not have begun

To Battin
Who talked so I could listen

To Bob
Who lives every day with me

WHAT I CANNOT SAY/I WILL SAY

IV/The Bell Is First Within Us

WHAT I CANNOT SAY/I WILL SAY

Perhaps you can imagine the girl
growing up in a house with no fireplace

Where she imagined the fireplace would be
there was a bookcase the size of a fireplace

and she reached into it year after year
taking out books.

The reading was quick; it consumed her.

She did other things slowly.
She went to sleep slowly and woke up the same way.

She took a long time with her dreams.

She began to read other things:
people's faces
deep weathered cracks on the backs of farmer's necks
the bleary eyes of the butcher

how the top soil lay to the south of town in winter
black as coal and glittering.

I/SPEAKING FROM THE BLOOD

SPEAKING FROM THE BLOOD

Speaking from the blood
I can no longer tell you
fear or fire or loss
but make a patience
out of all of these

woven.

Do not think of cloth
but of weaving
of the motion of weaving
which is to be thrown
back and forth like a shuttle
between two hands.

And then, once again
do not think of the shuttle
as something solid
but as the motion

of weaving.

PHOTOGRAPH

Here is Kate with feet.   And hands.
In the winter, children have faces;
in summer they have arms   and legs.
These grow on summer nights by
stretching them.   Some children
refuse to believe they cannot fly.
Crouching in the dark   they spread
their arms and leap

JOURNEY

The road ahead like
a tongue laid down
smoothly she unrolls
herself between
ground swell shape
on either side.

Close on the right
this woods: long needle
pine form ranks tight
to the range of her
eye; with her eye
round as a compass
she hears old warnings
about steps re-traced.
Her sense of direction
rises, coming to a point.

To the left some distance
a single stand of birch:
there, tangled as hair
rising in white shock
from deep roots splayed

out in dark
she comes up.

PHOTOGRAPH: MIDWEST CEMETERY

If you stood there long enough
in your black boots, dark figure,
would your name come up through
these feet, your roots, up into
your stem; would your name
come coursing then from out beyond,
would your mouth call out a name
older than the one you know
and say it as your own?

Who says your name at night,
taps you gently on the forehead:
the one whose sister took a
curling iron slip quick sizzle
and it's done, the last sound
her skin will ever make?

I know the midwest cemeteries
through my feet; they rise,
these stones, inevitable as
the prairie they come from
marking mounds of dead of living
of lives now lost to me.   I
know them all through my feet
and hands, too, I move
over stones reading names.

I want to know their names.
Naming who and what and when.
Does it matter out beyond
that we struggle to name their
names and try to know our own?
Who touches me gently
on the forehead in the night
and calls me up from sleep
through the dark
through the long tunneling stem
Who calls my name?

MEETING JOYCE'S PARENTS

I will tell you his name: it is Emil.
And so he says it
working from resonance
ringing inside his head
through teeth (these resist);
it rides out richly clad
in some other tongue's accent:
I am Emil.
There are trees on certain European boulevards
trimmed yearly, pruned for longevity;
this is Emil.
Spare; a long lean thrust into life,
his foliage is in the hands
the man is an artisan.

I cannot tell you hers —
she has a name
complex, subtle
by which she has never been called.
She reads the name as she breathes.
It is the nuance of her life.
When she held the child
moist, close, humming her life into its ear,
the breath nestled:
a secret, precise song
taking its shape from the coil
of a child's inner ear.
My ear, already attuned
to the timbre and quality
of that songchild/grown woman
listens now to the original score;
wonders at the symphony of the woman
whose name is nuance.

I see her suddenly now
in the same room, an Iris
evolved from the dark inner circle

of this parental eye.
She blooms unbearably.
Their triad makes a chord;
in this room it hangs
trembling before my eyes.
Emil, Nuance, and the child named Woman.
These two, the given tone; diminished.
She, perfect; augmented.

Saying goodby I am moved without warning
to rest my cheek on the cheek of the
woman who breathes; listening for what
I did not know.
Now, days later
humming
I lay down these words.

FOR LUETKA

There is nothing corporal
about this funeral; unless
you imagine the body within
has, through some
last effort to breathe,
caused the steel lid to
hump into that rounded curve.

I want to touch
what is removed from us,
what we remove ourselves from.
There is something
in these details:

That after this funeral,
returning to the home
she made with her sisters,
I saw four pans
stacked in the tub:
two of them plastic
from the five & dime;
one round stainless steel;
and a large pan from the farm,
oval and white chipped
with red enamel rim.

She died at home.
She who had a stroke
and could not speak
for 10 months,
heaved up her insides
at last
something moving
something coming out
through her throat
through her mouth

speaking to her sisters,
one who cannot hear
and one whose eyes fail her,
the two of them
catching her life
in these pans.

SWATHING

From the Tuesday, July 12 newspaper
of Douglas County & Alexandria, MN:

"Swathing, which for some farmers
began last week, is expected to be
in full swing this week."

We spend this week near
a strip of gravel road
cutting through two horizons
of flatland
planted with grain.
Walking that road in the morning
you hear acres of oats
pass the wind along
in fields of gold gone blanched;
the underside of pure color
confronting always
your inner eye.
Oh the sky has the color
mornings the sky is topside
riding high with color.
Afternoon brings it down.
Fields overtake the sky
haze ascends
and the grain goes ripe
with gold
rising up
brazen.

Swathing is expected this week.

WHAT COLOR IS OLD AND WHY DOES HER MUSIC FLY FROM MY THROAT LIKE A FLOCK OF WORDS?

Rutabaga is a good word, but what does it mean? Is it red? Does it root? Have you seen or eaten one? Not me. But I believe in them. I believe in the sound of rutabaga, and that there are Some, maybe not now or even lately, who know the rutabaga. Have pulled one resisting from the earth, dirt clinging, and know the smell. The chop, the boil, the chew of a rutabaga.

I could ask her about rutabagas. But it's never been like that. It's never been her handkerchiefs or her recipes or anything she's told me. Still, sure as a rutabaga, she knows it. Has pulled it, resisting, the whole length of her life. A substance. Stubborn, and a root, it is not easy to get hold of. Not for me. Not for her. But she's done it. Is still doing it. I am studying how. Even as I do it, I study her for how.

There's nothing to tell. The house is still there, white, a mansion with green gables and two turrets. The bed was in one of them. They tied rags to the bed posts for her to pull on. It was there she birthed my sister, my brother. She wasn't always a mother.

At age 33 I realized I was just 7 years from being 40. As I put it in a letter to her: years old, that is. I said: It's odd, aging. Something that happens to you from the outside. Not having anything to do with who we feel we are inside. Is it like that? I asked her in her 70's. She wasn't always old.

'Yes,' she wrote back.

But it's not from the telling I know it. It's from the house that was the hospital (before they built the hospital) still being there. After Pearl Harbor they sent away for a delivery table to be put in the new hospital. She birthed me on that, but preferred the bed. Pulling the cloth taut. So before the delivery table, there was the house with the bed. Still there. And before that, she was not a mother.

I wrote, looking at my face in the mirror in the morning during the night of my second baby: The bloom that is gone—where? Flushed down the toilet with thousands of rinsed diapers?

'You have a way of putting things,' she said.

Before her surgery I hold in my purse my mother's watch, the pearl ring my father gave her before they married. I see her, yesterday, turning the thin gold wedding band around her finger, saying: If they want this, they'll have to cut off another bone. Thwack! She throws her purse halfway across the room, landing it on the dresser.

A nurse appears: Your mother is fine. The doctor will see you now. We walk together. She chuckles, and says confidentially in an undertone: She is a fine woman.

Why confidential? Why in an undertone, not to be said too loudly in these sterile hallways? Would the nurse have said it to me more directly across the bed as she was untying rags from the bedpost after the birth of my sister before I was born?

At nine years of age, I am standing at the back door in a February thaw, noticing the Christmas wreath. Still hanging there. Valentine's Day, and she hasn't taken it down. I swing my foot. Poke the toe of my boot through a skin of ice refrozen over deep puddles. It cracks. My boot breaks through satisfying as any shattering: My mother is a strong woman.

Her eyes fly open. Wild. The anesthetic. She says: It was cold in there.

At the age of four, leaning over the banister of the choir left looking down, down into the long Cathedral aisle, I could tell the weddings from the funerals by the colors people wore. Dark or light. Like the music. Like the light coming through the high, round window, falling red, or blue, or yellow onto the organ. Her feet on the pedals long and wooden, curved beneath the stretch of her legs, like a first quarter moon: crescent. Her feet fly. Her hands fly. Back & forth, up & down over three tiers of keys. Ivory. Stopping only to flick a switch on either side; to the left, to the right, names of pipes: Woodwind; Tremulo; Trumpet. In the same moment, lifting her arm to direct the four voice choir facing her. Facing me. Watching. I have studied her for how.

Coming here in the car to care for my children, we had to stop five times for her to throw up. 79, she puzzled and lay on my couch, closing her eyes. While she slept my friend said to me: *five times?* (She had to get the number right.) And then: Oh—of course. Her baby is going half-way around the world.

I did. And arriving there, I had in my purse the address of a young woman, her student, who is an organist at the Cathedral in the city of my visit. 3,000 miles from that other curve of pedals, from the stops with the names of the pipes, from the old woman lying on the couch, puzzling, were the two of us: her student; her daughter. One at the organ. One at

23

the desk. Her fingers flew. The line of birthing. First, hers of me. But we were not always mothers. Back and forth. Up and down. Over three tiers of keys, and the typewriter is electric.

Rutabagas are not red: of the Swedish or yellow turnip.

Yellow. She turns toward the bank of tulips, and sighs: There are so many yellow ones this year.

'What do you mean?' I ask. (The word is good, but what does it mean?)

'No matter what colors you plant, eventually, over the years, they all come back yellow.'

IT IS FORBIDDEN TO NOTICE
THAT YOU ARE DYING

It is forbidden to notice
that you are dying,
to fall clear of your body,
to leave its veins
pumping, visible
in your upturned wrist;
forbidden to turn and watch
as you leave yourself

behind
behind

It is forbidden to inform yourself
of this death, or any death;
to know the form in life
is this shape
the one you turn and see;
to notice that you are living.

The alarm sounds
but you are already awake
in the light

and the light has always been forbidden.

II/A DARK RUSH OF GREEN

SOMETHING IS AT OUR HEELS

Something is at our heels
your heels, and mine;
I cannot make it out.
If I turn   it runs
amorphous, right behind
and wants us by the tail.

TRIPTYCH

I / PRELUDE

This is the poem
I avoid, coming to it
fingers fresh
from eight years
of one Bach Prelude:
played for two years;
played well for five;
played with teeth
for this last
and now heard it
for the first time
come from my fingers
playing itself—
this poem I avoid
about opening a window
in the basement
reaching up
to open a window
and nothing but screen
between me and grass growing
overhead; nothing but
wall holding back
earth   I can smell
how black it is
and do not want
to write this poem.

II / LABOR

I lament this blindness
in the same voice
my grandmother used
to tell how much
she paid the doctor
to tend a favorite
complaint. Over & over

I say: This blindness
follows me everywhere—no—
arrives just before I do.
I cannot see. And today
the compensation began:

the quickening
of another sense.
Tapping my way through
the kitchen, the evening
meal   I began
to listen for sounds
that cannot be heard:

the sound of a heart attack
of an orgasm
of a muscular movement
signaling death
or pleasure
or   yes
the onset of labor.

III / BIRTH

When the amniotic sac breaks
you are opened   it begins
a warm rush of fluid   you
are amazed: blood   water
you cannot stop   you
didn't know this birthing
would make you breathe
now   now
would be so final
like a death   bearing down
you are surprised at the
small crown of head   hair
mixing with your own
private   wet pain.

These are details
you do not forget.
Alert, you begin to miss
animals you have never known:
the sight of yellowed teeth
(soft curling lip folded back);
your hands know the absence
of hair   stiff, bristled;
you finger leaves from
the burning bush at your back door
pink and supple as inner skin.
The color rises   almond shaped
into flaming tongues.

You dream you have given birth
to the head of a child:
male or female remains
in the body, but you know
it will be both.

LETTER TO THE
WEDDING PHOTOGRAPHER,
NINE YEARS LATER

Sir: Nine years ago today sometime between
the hours of 12 noon and one—your camera jammed;
it began recording events in montage
making multiple images.
The day I was a bride, your camera
took pictures of my brain.
My brain jammed today;
it began showing slides of my wedding day
personal incisive images of feelings
textures   how the light fell.
At 10:30 this morning my third girlchild
slips from my hands into tubwater
I see her go   legs   buttocks   back
pink   firm

    I am plunged naked into the basement of a cathedral
    in half light standing there before stones the color of my skin
    I raise my arms into satin, white. I am so thin; so cold.
    The air watches me in my solitude. Listen: People arriving
    overhead. Gusts of jubilance wash down the stairwells
    I will wait
    I will wait
    until the church swallows them all.
    11:15 and I am caught on the stairwell
    one foot on each step; hands a clutch of material
    it is slippery and I like my hands full of it

But I am making sandwiches
slicing an apple
the radio plays Greensleeves
"... and who but my Lady named ..."

    the flagstones of that vestibule floor
    I name them grey and hardly stand in white cloth shoes
    I see only the tips of my shoes on this flagstone floor

and next to those tips my father's protrude, black & shiny.
I am not aware of any substance; should I take his arm
(and I will) my fingers will pass right through it.
I brace myself for what I will hear next

And at 11:45 today everything present stops existing
the air is grand; it waits with me. For 15 minutes
I wait for what I will hear next.
I am standing at the bathroom sink
this washcloth   I wash here everyday
the washcloth is green
the spigot is on

> *and bells splash into my brain*
> *bells ringing   air alive with*
> *music.   Rossini.   It is the March*
> *the music, the bells that I cannot*
> *bear to hear   and I can hear them.*

Standing squarely awash with tears
I listen fiercely from these married years.
I develop constantly
the imprints of that day
and I say, Sir,
this goes beyond photographs.

A DARK RUSH OF GREEN

Looking up, I see them
standing in shade
the three of them
talking together
young girls
seven, eight, and nine.
They do not know
that I watch
from up out of my woman's body
that I see
their easy, early stance
and how the deep shade
moves over them
slowly fanning
first one, then another
with a dark rush of green.

I remember how yesterday
I found them up against the wall
just inside the door of
this resort's pool hall
where they weren't supposed
to go: (old men from the town
come to drink beer and play).
This time coming through the door
from acres of sun out there
to dark in here
I sense before I see
the throb of adolescence
the ache and burst of it
pulsing, pushing at walls.
And there, these three standing
with arms crossed.
Seven, eight, and nine
they stand close,
leaning into the pulse
searching for its shape.

They turn on me.
The eyes of the eight-year-old
fly at me, flailing.
She can see, they all can see
I know the shape; have
assumed and discarded it.
Not like these others
who are the shape.
These others who will give
the shape to them.

So now,
from up out of my woman's body
I see first one, then another
in a dark rush of green.

THE UNICORN

That Christmas some men
almost stole everything
from the house two doors
down. There was a break
in. We went the next night
to a small noisy gathering
with children, with friends
to exchange   gifts.
That Christmas I received
a bowl filled with ever
green (I wrote my cousin
I said: I'm breaking
out)   and the children
roared around. In the bowl
under the evergreen was:
an eggshell cracked wide
open, five rhinestones stuck
to its insides halfway down;
bits of feather;   bone
chocolate covered cherries;
a single red pellet dropping
down;   one yellow ball and
nuts.   We left
our house with lights on
and music for the burglars
if they called
if they tried
to steal our christmas
while we were out with friends
while I read aloud *A Child's
Christmas in Wales*, in Minnesota.
I gave a reading
in my husband's vest
the one he wore when
we married each other so long
ago, before feathers and bones
from some tiny bird lay broken

in the bottom of a round clay
bowl.   I read to Joyce
in her new silk scarf; and Soren
in his mother's lap. In his
mother's lap and crying
from afar off up high crying
children's voices   My voice
reading.   It's all I should be
doing.   From morning to night
reading aloud to gatherings.
To burglars.   To men
who are not my husband.
To children in and out
of laps.   To women holding
bowls full of feathers and
bones.   When we got home
the music was playing
to a house no one else can rob.
The unicorn is already here
taking everything.

THE BUSINESS DINNER POEM I

I do not like the woman
who flashes her rings,
her teeth, falsely;
or the man in his soft
skin calling his son
names, not naming
his wife.

I like the house.
Its thin wooden bones
cradle me in narrow halls,
propel me forward through
arched openings into
full-bellied rooms.

In this house I think of
the woman who wears stitches
like teeth in an old cut
at the base of her throat;
of the man who was able
to say what he meant.

In this house
it is clear that some,
sensing movement,
gather rocks and hiss;
others putting on skin
etched with amulets
go out to meet it.

A WHITE PLACE

Things are small
in this room:

—These three
old shaving brushes
contain decades of
bristle bent to cheek.
Your father's mornings
stretching backward
roll and curl off
the white-lined horizon
of these walls.
In this light
your beard is fierce
red.

—And again
this small black box
exquisite; a replica
of married years
stark naked black
in this very large
white, the box
contains your ring.
Things are contained
here; but in this room
things are small.

The space is large; here
you could unwrap your arms
from around your body
and rage.

There is room.

40

PIECES

The paper is
whole
expensive.

She lifts the paper
in the daylight
in the 3rd floor studio;
tears the paper.

It must make a sound:
this tearing apart.

I know the sound.
Treading the day
in another house
I feel the sound
daily
torn
into fragments
like the paper
she works with

now in pieces
awaiting the sacrament of paint;
the anointing of the edge.
Pigments (fleshcolored or blue
like blood before it hits the air)
are poured, saturating
especially the torn place.

The wound steeps itself in color.

AFTER THE READING

The dentist tells me
I grind my teeth
in my sleep.
He looks at me
closely   hoping
I won't be embarrassed
he found tension
in my life.   He is young
quick (visions of fawn
body rotting off the road
slam through my brain)
so I do not tell him

That I play this tension
trading in teeth for my life.
That I chew dream hides
until I can wear them
like skin.   That I appear
wearing only this skin
before an audience
reading aloud.

That nothing will help:
not eating fish
not wearing suede
not tongues of iris.

That I stand
facing North in the summer;
That some frightened animal
runs before me in the forest
unseen   ahead

THE STORY

There was something about you
telling me the story of the man
who tracked the white wolf

something at variance
between the story and your face
ruddy, genteel

coming from generations
of men who wore patience
like a kind of grape
bottled into fine wine

men who studied
the nuance of weather and sun
which slope; learning
how long it takes to ripen

something about this
cultivation in your face

at odds with the words
you began to choose
to tell me the story

of the man
who gave himself gradually
to the ways of the wolf

took on his habits
ate his food

something about the motion
of your fingers showing me how
he dug in the snow
in the arctic cold and wild

howling

something about howling
your face has forgotten
but the words have not

the words move in your fingers

tell us one more time
the story of how

we ate raw meat
wore skins
lived in a cave

believed in the dark

III/INTO THE MIRROR

SHE IS SAYING

a dancing
movement back
and forth; the
shell hanging
in my window
trembles
in a wave
of sound moving
from the motor
in the bus
to concrete below
up the wall of my house
into the glass and
this shell
surprised and transparent
breaks
into a million seconds.
My neighbor
says she believes
this turn in the weather
has come
because they went
to the moon.
Sound enters my arms
my legs, beginning
the pleasure
of random movement
and someone is saying:
a dancing
a moving back
and forth

TRAVELING TOWARD PICASSO
THROUGH GERTRUDE STEIN

Picasso.
What did I see here?
I see the man himself
looking out
through his eyes
the man in his studio
his eyes
the man
in the great space of his studio
the great space in the man
his studio
his eyes
the man with his hand
in the bowels of the lamb
the beast
the bull
horns
laughing
the man with his bite
on the fish
swimming
looking up, down
sideways & inside
simultaneously
the man
laughs
he thinks
he laughs
he draws
and paints this thinly
hardly covers up
the thin line
between seeing
and laughing
loud uproarious
color

pushing out
cubes—no—
space
the line forever broken
line moved aside
to make space
there is room
in this man for us all
and the only thing I see
like Stein
is Picasso
Yes
Thank you.

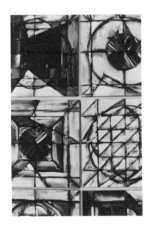

INTO THE MIRROR

From out of a mansion
this old mirror stands
floor to ceiling, placed
on the stairway landing
as our third child, a girl,
is about to be born.
Often walking down steps
toward this mirror I
catch the thought of
my children, all girls,
falling into the mirror.
This fear is not so strong
for myself, but
it sometimes happens
the heel catches
you go careening toward
could fall through:
the head
the shoulders
smashing into glass
falling through your own image
the force of your self
shattering
the image.
For myself
my children, all girls,
I have this fear
of the possibility of
death by fractured image.

ASH WEDNESDAY

I am trying to remember
dust, not that I am
dust, or unto dust
but what was done
to me in the name of
dust. Some kind of

burning took place
in my father's furnace
beginning in the fall
in the name of the father
men brought coal in trucks
and sent it down the chute
into the bin in the basement
with no warning, no call
to say they were coming,
or knock on the door;
just that sudden
terrible violation
of sound in a house
where I lived alone
during the day
with my mother

and watched silence
fall into itself
like folds
in the lap of my skirt
as I sat, mornings
on the floor, playing
or singing, I can still
hear my own voice and
the silence in that house.

This was a small town
but I didn't know the men

or the truck they drove up
onto the lawn, next to the window
the living room window, and
beneath it, the opening:
they were heaving shovels
into an opening
in my house

there was a way
large men in thick coats
who said nothing, could come
and hit a house with waves of coal;
could stand as if they belonged there
slamming noise into a house.

No one told me.

No one man I had for a father
no woman, my mother, said:
"Men who say nothing, will come
bringing coal for the furnace.
It will be sudden and violent."

I saw this was followed
by the burning
every night, a roaring fire
stoked by my father who never told me
and after the fire begun in the fall
that burned through the winter
there were ashes, and toward spring

these ashes appeared in a cup
held in the palm of another man
this one dressed
to look as if he weren't a man
and I thought he wasn't a man
so the shock of his thumb
dry and warm on my forehead
pressing ashes into it as if
he knew me personally, intoning:

Remember *thou art dust*
and unto dust thou shalt return
is the closest I came
to anyone telling me anything.

FOR KATE

Five year old
you leap through
mornings
fingers splayed
like an arpeggio.

In late afternoon
you bring your young deer
legs unsteady
to my lap

and tell me her sounds
how she hides in the closet
has no place of her own
will never grow up.

I stroke the deer
stroke the deer.
You say: Mama
this is no game.

I nod in rhythm
stroking
stroking
the light falls away.

Pulling the kitchen
around us, we sit.
Others come in
for dinner.

RITUAL

I go around the house at night
turning on all the lights.
During one ordinary minute
of an afternoon's edge, day
shuts down slam into dusk.

Moving in ancient ritual
I make a procession
from room to room
lamp to lamp.

The child in my arm
sleeps then startles.
New circles of light
stretch into her dream.

Bigger children dance, and
jingling, jump at their shadows
catching or caught
they fly at the dark
dancing in circles and circles of light.

I meet the night out each window
as I pass by   we stare
and nod acknowledging the ancient pact.

At the door of the cave
I light the lights.
I tend the fire.
Soon the father will be back
filling the doorway with his shoulders.

YOU & I MEET

You & I meet
in front of a bakery
on the street
of a European city
neither of us
has been in before.

Strangers, coming
from opposite directions,
we pause and reach
instinctively
for the other.

I know the way.
Touching immediately
your most intimate part
you rise in response
filling me

all of this while we
are moving   we
have hardly paused
in our travel
through the opposite direction
of each other.

On a shelf in the window
next to tiny baskets
of French marzipan
our third child
stirs in her sleep.
Everything is safe and foreign.

NAKED

grandma serves
sliced peaches
carefully skinned
slippery

Kate says:
why don't we have this
at home?
what, I say, don't we
have at home
she laughs

naked peaches

and says to each one
shouting: I'm eating
a naked peach

naked wiggles up
out of her throat
laughing

my mother
my father
her mother
her father
all confronted
with naked
with peach

that round ball
de-furred; laid open
each stone coaxed
from its red center
that globe cut
into yellow slices
of moon   my mother

who created all this
my daughter
who gives me the words
and I
who write them down

what a trinity
we make.

THE BUSINESS DINNER POEM II

When you are a woman
in your mid-thirties
having been raised
in Minnesota having studied
music as a child
having learned at the edge
of each small town
the prairie begins;
when you are
this kind of woman
in your mid-thirties you know
how to survive.

You know
how not to ask
the old man
who fought in the fields
outside Paris
if he killed anyone.

You know how
to let him talk
about silk stockings
and cigarettes for 5¢ a pack
let him talk (his face hung
like an English sheepdog)
making jokes about men older
than he is, relieved
there are some.
You nod, soon forty.

You know, having survived
winters you clearly remember
how to dance and talk:
you can outlast any weather
with the proper gear.

Being a woman
in your thirties you know
how to let the music carry you;
how to listen to a man
who will not talk;
how not to let the core
inside the last note slip down
before you have gutted it
with your teeth
and planted the seed
against another winter.

OUT OF MY HANDS

This is not the time to write
not now when my daughter's clavicle
is pushing to define itself
raised like a braille I can read
with my eyes closed.

This is her collarbone; this her chin
here her cheekbones: I am telling you
all of this from my fingers where
the memory of what I see daily
resides.   It rides in my hands
as if I myself had fashioned the
slow spread of these bones   as if
by tending her hours I have somehow
become architect of this new form.

It is not so.

All I did was look at the lashes
lowered over her father's eyes and
touch the light blue place beneath them
where the skin pulses to the beat
of a heart.   After that it was our breath
moving through the whole length of our bodies
like a shudder

that became her collarbone.

IV/THE BELL IS FIRST WITHIN US

NO

As a child   I was given to lying down
belly flat on bridges and easing myself over
'til I hung upside down to see what was
underneath.   (Troll.   I'm talking to you)
Another thing I used to do   was sit
on top of refrigerators. You might think
I have made that up to entertain you:
I have not.   My mother would say:

Monica   Come down off that refrigerator   Right Now.

No.

What are you doing up there?

Looking. I like how things look from up here.

You've had your look. Come Down.

No.

TURN

But now
I turn

in my sleep
like the dog

and forget
everything

but that moment
of the hare

frozen in flight
against snow

and my first leap
in hunger.

Now I twitch
in my sleep

like the dog
and dream

of the hare
and my leap

EDGE

I am in the cockpit
of this plane, —no
not this plane
but another one.
The captain is not
the Chicago Italian
flying this plane;
the captain is French
with small exquisite feet
in big boots
working the rudders
and we know, he and I,
that everything
is freezing up out there.
It is a moment
of no enemy planes
but war is
and I am exposed
riding like this
thrust forward
into the vacuum
created by two engines
two propellers.
I depend on the wing
and riding the wing
is some dark shape
lean as a hound.
"Bark, damn you,
there's fog out there,"
the Frenchman shouts
lifting his hands
to wave this black dog
to attention.
I look down at my wrist
where the pulse bumps along
through one blue vein.
The plane lifts

and above our heads
there is a break
a clear line
where fog ends
and sky begins.
It is possible
in this plane I am in
and also in the other one
I said I was not in
to ride this line
half in, half out
of fog
half in, half out
of sky.
It is possible
to ride, to land
to believe I am no longer
in a vacuum, that when
I step out of a plane
I have something solid
under my feet.
I can believe all this
if I want to
or if I have to
but for me it is always
that moment
when I am exposed
riding like this
thrust forward
into the vacuum.

DREAMS COME AND INHABIT US

We have no choice
We cannot say:
I will never sleep again

We have to sleep
and when we sleep
dreams come.

We cannot say
yes or no

Dreams come.

Hunger Jones stood   on the southwest plains   in Minnesota
put her hands on her hip   made a crook of her arm   Looked

at the silo tipped toward the sky   at the horse leaning
on its legs   at the iron clapper   inside the bell   Made

a move with her foot   put it down in the field   Remembered
the dear black absence of land   in the hold of an immigrant

ship   Felt the waves   coming in acres   land was an island
they called Ellis   and other words she couldn't say   Her

tongue thick with the split   of every bond she'd known
this keening   that rang through her   shank to bone.

BELL

for R.M.B who told me
and for his father before him

Listen to how
a bell is cast (as we all are)
with muttering and clanking
formed in the dark, and
raised to sound.

We think we cannot bear it
the ringing of the bell.
I thought this on my wedding day
and wrote it down nine years later
I said: It is the bells
I cannot bear to hear and
I can hear them.

We cannot make a thing
that does not reflect our
selves, and we have made
the bell.   So we must
contain it.   The bell
is first within us.

Hearing the bells we have made
we hear the size of our selves
and think   we cannot bear it

We tell ourselves we were not meant
to ring   and when the vibrations
begin: a birthing   a death
the sound of another's voice
light/shadow   any blade of grass

When the wave of these occasions
begins   we are afraid
we think we were not meant to ring
We do not move naturally (the

containers)   instead we think
we must contain it   and since
we cannot   the sound of the bells
we have made   is too much for us
Hearing them ring   we know instinctively
we are the bell   but we are afraid
that if we ring   our eardrums will burst
from the inside out   We say:

This is too much   because we are trying
to contain it   and when the wave
hits us   the pain   the joy   if we
are dying   or being born   we think
we were not made   for this much pain
or this much joy   and the bell peals
or the bell tolls   and we cannot bear it
because we have waited for the bell
to tell us: this death   this marriage
this christening   this calamity

When in fact   as it happens
I sit by the side of the old man
in the hospital where the nurse
tells me   He is living   but his hand
closed around mine says   He is dying
and the pull of it   wakes me   mid-night
his white torso   propped on a bed
that bends in on itself   is hollowing
from the inside out: my shape
your shape   his shape

or   as it happens   A big man
bends toward me   kissing the top
of my head   where babies crown
when they are born   Saying a name
like a christening

or   as it happens
I say a word to you   and you
say the same word to me   not
from your mouth   or even from the back
toward your throat   but from midway

inside it   deep and playful   ringing

and this is how it happens
these first vibrations   a wave
and when we feel ourselves begin
to sound with it   we are afraid   we say:
This is only snow   or   this is a leaf
when in fact the Eskimos had many names
one for a snow that will stay   one
that will go   for the powder   for
the crust;   the Indians a name for the leaf
when it buds   another for the unfolding
a name for its burst into color
but here is the one   The Indians had
a name   there was a name   for
that moment when the leaf falls

and the great occasion   of each leaf
falling   happens in silence
until suddenly we notice   the
floor of the forest is covered
and the wind whips them up   all
before our eyes   like the roar
of the bells we have made   sounding
the event before our ears

But we are the event
happening   now   in silence   a falling
into pain   into joy so large
only we   the bell   can sound with it
moving back birth forth death   not
between them   sounding them

we think we will crack   break   but
we will not   It is only the
vibrations moving through us
the wave of our selves   sounding

we hold the size of it happening
the cadence   the range of our selves
deeply struck   the sound disperses
leaves us   trembling

73

WHAT I CANNOT SAY

I have hills at either hand
dark hulking shapes
close as chairs in a child's night
draped with clothes

and in between
fields curve
like the belly
of a white beluga whale
in a well-muscled turn
sweeping upward
to break surface.

At night the fields float
like souls rising.
What I cannot say tonight
I will say and say and say

It lights   like fire
off the pile of kindling:
your bones collapsed
into a bare stick heap.

This burns out of holes
that held your eyes
and what I cannot say
I will say, one word
after another, put down
like feet to the road.

Something red runs
in the marrow of my bones;
something that even cracked open
will not drip out, but vibrates
like a string pulled taut
over the violin's bridge.

When there is no meat
and the teeth are gone;
nothing to tear at
nothing to tear with

When beyond flesh
your mouth gapes at me

When there are no wolves
and nothing runs wild;
past the snap
of fresh green beans
cut into the bowl
between my mother's knees

the birds have pecked the juice
from every raspberry propped
on tall sticks at the garden's back

the garden with its back to me

This shivering—

What is red does not keep me warm.
I am cold and swimming;
and what I cannot say
I will say.

Monica Ochtrup grew up in southwestern Minnesota: in the Sleepy Eye Public Library; under her mother's grand piano; watching fields out the window of her father's '51 Ford. Presently she lives and writes in St. Paul where she and Bob Ochtrup raise three daughters: Jennifer, Heidi, and Kate. She is Poetry Editor for the *WARM Journal. What I Cannot Say/I Will Say* is her first collection of poems.

photo by Bob Ochtrup

THE MINNESOTA VOICES PROJECT

#18 Neal Bowers, THE GOLF BALL DIVER (poems), $3.50

Jonis Agee, and others, eds. BORDER CROSSINGS: A MINNESOTA VOICES PROJECT READER, $8.00

The Fourth Annual Competition

#19 Margaret Hasse, STARS ABOVE, STARS BELOW (poems), $3.50

#20 C. J. Hribal, MATTY'S HEART (short stories) $6.00

#21 Sheryle Noethe, THE DESCENT OF HEAVEN OVER THE LAKE (poems), $3.50

#22 Monica Ochtrup, WHAT I CANNOT SAY/I WILL SAY (poems) $3.50

Copies of any or all of these books may be purchased directly from the publisher by filling out the coupons below and mailing it, together with a check for the correct amount and $1.00 per order for postage and handling, to:

New Rivers Press
1602 Selby Ave.
St. Paul, MN 55104

Please send me the following books: _____

_____

_____

_____

_____

_____

I am enclosing $_____ (which includes $1.00 for postage and handling) Please send these books as soon as possible to:

NAME _____

ADDRESS _____

CITY & STATE _____

ZIP _____